James Russell Lowell, John Greenleaf Whittier

Tributes to William Lloyd Garrison

At the Funeral Services, May 28, 1879

James Russell Lowell, John Greenleaf Whittier

Tributes to William Lloyd Garrison
At the Funeral Services, May 28, 1879

ISBN/EAN: 9783744659765

Printed in Europe, USA, Canada, Australia, Japan

Cover: Foto ©ninafisch / pixelio.de

More available books at **www.hansebooks.com**

TRIBUTES

TO

WILLIAM LLOYD GARRISON,

AT THE

FUNERAL SERVICES,

MAY 28, 1879.

BOSTON:

HOUGHTON, OSGOOD AND COMPANY.

The Riverside Press, Cambridge.

1879.

THE announcement of the critical illness of Mr. Garrison, speedily followed by that of his death while absent from home, took his friends and the public on both sides of the Atlantic by surprise ; for though it was known that he had long been infirm in health, the vigor of his recent contributions to the public press (the latest of which, in denunciation of the Anti-Chinese Bill, and on the exodus of the freedmen from Mississippi and Louisiana to Kansas, had appeared within a few weeks) had made it difficult to believe that his health was at all precarious. Only his family and immediate friends knew that those letters were written while he was suffering such pain and discomfort that the feeling that he must lift up his voice, and bear his testimony once more on the question of human rights, alone enabled him to accomplish the task. The exhaustion and prostration which followed these efforts made it evident to himself that his forces were nearly spent, and gave his family much concern.

Even from Mr. Garrison's seventy-third birthday (December 10, 1878), his private letters were marked by forebodings of his approaching end, which he welcomed as a relief from his physical infirmities. In the following April, 1879, the feeling which he described as a giving way of the internal organism became so strong, and his malady (a chronic affection of the kidneys) so intolerable, that, at the solicitation of his daughter, he went to New York to put himself under the care of her family physician. He arrived at the Westmoreland Apartment House, where she resided, on Monday afternoon, April 28th. On Wednesday the treatment began, with immediate promise of good results, which was, however, of necessity soon disappointed. On Saturday, May 10th, Mr. Garrison took to his bed, but even then those about him did not fairly realize the gravity of his condition. At the end of another week, however, the symptoms became unmistakably alarming, and on Tuesday, May 20th, the members of the family in Boston were summoned by telegraph and arrived the next day. The final changes proceeded slowly, and the death-struggle did not set in till half-past ten o'clock on the evening of Friday. Up to that time Mr. Garrison, though disinclined to talk unless spoken to, or to indicate his wants, retained all his faculties, and recognized his children and grandchildren by voice and by sight; and only an hour or two before he lost this consciousness, he listened with manifest pleasure to the singing of his favorite hymns, to which, as he lay outstretched, he beat time both with his hands and feet. He expired peacefully at a few minutes past eleven o'clock on the succeeding night, Saturday, May 24th. His illness had been in many respects a distressing one, even in comparison with the wretched months that preceded it; but the prevailing sense was of weariness — frequently expressed in a desire to " go home " — rather than of acute bodily pain, though that was not wanting. His vitality was remarkably illustrated through-out.

A post-mortem examination having been made on Mon-day, Mr. Garrison's remains were removed the same night to Roxbury, Mass. On Wednesday afternoon, May 28th, the funeral services were held in the neighboring church of the First Religious Society, which the Trustees had kindly placed at the disposal of the family and the public. At sunset the body was interred beside that of Mrs. Garrison in the cemetery at Forest Hills.

William Lloyd Garrison.

Born in Newburyport, Mass., December 10, 1805.

Died in New York City, May 24, 1879.

FUNERAL

OF

WILLIAM LLOYD GARRISON.

EXERCISES AT THE CHURCH.

THE large assemblage which filled the spacious church
of the First Religious Society in Roxbury, on the occasion
of Mr. Garrison's funeral, was remarkable for the number
of his surviving friends and co-laborers in the Anti-Slavery
and kindred reformatory movements which it embraced;
and besides these there were present many of the race to
whose redemption from bondage he had consecrated his
best years, and not a few who were formerly indifferent or
hostile to the cause which he advocated, but who now desired to pay their tribute of respect and admiration to his
memory. In accordance with Mr. Garrison's views of death,
everything was done to avoid the appearance of mourning
or gloom. The blinds were opened to admit the cheerful
light of the perfect spring day; the pulpit was tastefully
decorated with flowers; and the hymns of cheer and inspiration of which he had been so fond were sung. The whole
audience rose when, a few minutes after two o'clock, the
body was borne into the church, attended by the pall-
bearers and followed by the family. The pall-bearers were

Wendell Phillips, Samuel May, Samuel E. Sewall, Robert F. Wallcut, Theodore D. Weld, Oliver Johnson, Lewis Hayden, and Charles L. Mitchell.

Rev. SAMUEL MAY opened the exercises by repeating the Lord's Prayer, and reading the following selections from the Old and New Testaments, some of which had been favorite quotations with Mr. Garrison, and often read by him at Anti-Slavery meetings.

"Shall not the Judge of all the earth do right?"

"The souls of the righteous are in the hand of God."
"He is not the God of the dead, but of the living."

"The Mighty God, even the Lord, hath spoken, and called the earth from the rising of the sun to the going down thereof.

"Hear, O my people, and I will speak; O Israel, and I will testify against thee.

"What hast thou to do to declare my statutes, or that thou shouldest take my covenant in thy mouth? Seeing thou hatest instruction, and castest my words behind thee.

"When thou sawest a thief, then thou consentedst with him, and hast been partaker with adulterers.

"Behold, the hire of the laborers who have reaped down your fields, which is of you kept back by fraud, crieth: and the cries of them who have reaped are entered into the ears of the Lord of Sabaoth."

"I, the Lord, love justice, I hate robbery for burnt offering."

"What mean ye that ye beat my people to pieces, and grind the faces of the poor? saith the Lord God of hosts."

"Bring no more vain oblations: incense is an abomination unto me; it is iniquity, even the solemn meeting.

"And when ye spread forth your hands I will hide mine eyes

from you ; yea, when ye make many prayers I will not hear: your hands are full of blood."

" Wherefore hear the word of the Lord, ye scornful men, that rule this people. Because ye have said, We have made a covenant with death, and with hell are we at agreement ; when the overflowing scourge shall pass through, it shall not come unto us.

" Therefore, thus saith the Lord : Judgment will I lay to the line, and righteousness to the plummet; and the hail shall sweep away the refuge of lies, and the waters shall overflow the hiding-place.

" And your covenant with death shall be disannulled, and your agreement with hell shall not stand ; when the overflowing scourge shall pass through, then ye shall be trodden down by it."

" Cry aloud, spare not; lift up thy voice like a trumpet, and show my people their transgression."

" None calleth for justice, nor any pleadeth for truth : they trust in vanity and speak lies: . . . .

" Their feet run to evil, and they make haste to shed innocent blood ; their thoughts are thoughts of iniquity : . . . .

" The way of peace they know not ; they have made them crooked paths. . . . .

" Judgment is turned away backward, and justice standeth afar off : truth is fallen in the street, and equity cannot enter.

" Yea, truth faileth ; and he that departeth from evil maketh himself a prey."

" So thou, O Son of Man, I have set thee a watchman unto the house of Israel ; therefore thou shalt hear the word at my mouth and warn them from me.

" When I say unto the wicked, O wicked man, thou shalt surely die ; if thou dost not speak to warn the wicked from his way, that wicked man shall die in his iniquity ; but his blood will I require at thine hand.

" Nevertheless, if thou warn the wicked of his way, to turn from it; if he do not turn from his way, he shall die in his iniquity; but thou hast delivered thy soul."

" The Spirit of the Lord God is upon me ; because He hath sent me to bind up the broken-hearted, to proclaim liberty to the captives, and the opening of the prison to them that are bound."
" Put away the evil of your doings from before mine eyes. Cease to do evil ; learn to do well ; seek justice ; relieve the oppressed ; judge the fatherless ; plead for the widow."
Then,
" Though your sins be as scarlet, they shall be as white as snow ; though they be red like crimson, they shall be as wool."

" When the ear heard me, then it blessed me ; and when the eye saw me, it gave witness to me ;
" Because I delivered the poor that cried, and the fatherless, and him that had none to help him.
" The blessing of him that was ready to perish came upon me."

" I know that my Vindicator liveth, and will stand up at length on the earth ; and in my flesh shall I see God.
" Yea, I shall see Him my friend."

" The righteous live forevermore ; their reward also is with the Lord ; and the care of them is with the Most High.
" Therefore shall they receive a glorious kingdom. . . . . For with His right hand shall He cover them ; and with His arm shall He protect them."
And Jesus said : —
" Inasmuch as ye have done it unto one of the least of these, my brethren, YE HAVE DONE IT UNTO ME."

" Him that overcometh will I make a pillar in the temple of my God. . . . . And I will write upon him my new name."

REMARKS OF REV. SAMUEL MAY.

" Mr. Garrison is dead " are words which have gone from mouth to mouth of many thousands, on both sides the ocean, during the last few days, and the fact will long continue to be a theme in many circles for sorrowful and yet joyful discourse, for pain mingled with deepest gratitude to the Divine Providence whose hand had so often been put forth for his deliverance, and brought him at last to a good old age, crowning his life with loving kindness and tender mercies ; surrounding him, at home and abroad, with " honor, love, obedience, troops of friends."

Thanksgiving and praise, from all our hearts, unto God, for all his goodness and favor to this his servant.

It is pleasant now to know that that name which, within the memory of most of us, was everywhere cast out as evil, loaded with bitter reproach, spoken with fear and hate, and regarded as synonymous with all that was dangerous and destructive, is now, may I not almost say, everywhere honored ; is now well-nigh universally regarded with enthusiastic admiration.

A great life has closed, — has closed its earthly stage and scenes, — and passed beyond our mortal sight. But never before was that life more potent for good than at this moment ; never before did he live, as he lives now : lives in the laws of the land, lives in a renovated Constitution, lives in the hearts of all true lovers of our country and of mankind, lives in the labors of those who are seeking to purge our land from the curse of Intemperance and rescue the legions who are now in slavery to intoxicating drink, lives in all the aspirations and hopes of those who seek the full recognition of Woman as man's equal in right and citizenship.

For death does not narrow the influence of such a life, but enlarges it; it gives the last needful pressure to the weight which stamps its image ineffaceably in history and upon humanity.

His friends do not gather around his lifeless body to-day to utter mere eulogies. Most of all they come to shower their blessings upon his name; to rejoice together for him; to thank God for his simple, strong, pure, true life, and for the grand work he has done, — done so steadfastly, so persistently, so fearlessly, done so well.

What a task was before him when he, then little more than a boy, first stood with American Slavery face to face! Three millions of slaves in the land, so grown from less than half a million under the fostering wings of the American Republic; a compact body of slaveholders, acting as with one will, and commanding the allegiance of state, of church, and of all political parties; a Constitution, which, as Daniel Webster affirmed of it, " recognized slavery and gave it solemn guarantees," while all the lesser political lights, and seemingly all the people, said Amen; — all these, and whatever else can be described or imagined of intellectual, commercial, social, individual force, were arrayed against the rash man who should speak against Slavery. What could one young man do? — a stripling David, without weapons, unless *the truth* and *the right* might be called weapons, and comparatively few then thought they would help him much.

" But I could not turn a deaf ear to the cries of the slaves," he said; " nor throw off the obligations which my Creator had fastened upon me. Yet I trembled, and exclaimed in the language of Jeremiah, ' Ah, Lord God! behold I cannot speak; for I am a child.' "

Then he reflected whose was the might, whose was the power, by which such work is done; and that in such a contest, "one shall chase a thousand, and two put ten thousand to flight."

Then came the determination, the solemn, high resolve to do and to give all he was and could. Then were spoken those words which, in themselves, are his immortal monument: "I am in earnest. I will not equivocate — I will not excuse — I will not retreat a single inch — *and I will be heard.*"

Oh! see his faith; see his absolute trust in Eternal Truth.

And now the whole life of this true-souled man rises clear, majestic, serene, in beautiful proportions, before our riveted, our fascinated gaze! How the theme tempts me on! But I must forbear, and let others here guide your thoughts, cheer your aching hearts, and lift your eyes upward and onward.

Should I speak at all of his personal character, it would be of those traits in which the world, who knew him least, has least believed. He was the very soul of good-will and helpfulness to every one who needed his helping hand, and was never too busy to give it. I must not speak much of his tender care and thoughtfulness for his wife and children; nor of the full blessing which they have borne back into his bosom. In the long illness of her who was struck down suddenly at his side, her efficient help at once withdrawn and henceforth to depend wholly on others, how did he give days and nights, and weeks and years, to be her solace, nurse, and comforter; and always cheerful, for her sake. May I, without suspicion of being biased by relationship, say here that the late Samuel J. May loved him for forty years, and to his latest earthly moment, with a brother's warmest love, which never cooled or changed, and claim the fact as good evidence for them both?

Who shall rightly set forth his life's work?

Here, to-day, I can only say that he was, in the highest sense, the faithful servant of God; and join my thanksgiving with yours for all he was: —

That he hearkened to the divine voice in his soul;

That he allowed no favor to blind, no fear to deter him;

That he spoke without reserve the truth as he saw it, and with the plainest utterance he could give it;

That his words became as those of a prophet in their piercing power;

That he walked amidst perils and deadly enemies unharmed, and that he saw his work fully vindicated in the sight of man; that, in the flesh, he saw God's law triumphant, saw the abolition of slavery, saw nearly four millions of slaves in his native land made freemen, and saw the general concurrence of all the nation's true and good in the needful amendment of the nation's organic law.

Dear friend, brave, true, good man, farewell! Lion-hearted when any wrong was to be rebuked and resisted, but the soul of patience, forbearance, and tenderness when sorrowing, suffering, or struggling hearts needed cheer and counsel, — farewell for now!

Yet while we speak our farewells we seem nearer to thee, surer of thee, than ever, and know that every motion of thy enlarged spirit beats — and will forever beat — in behalf of freedom and truth, for peace on earth and good-will among men.

"Servant of God, well done! Well hast thou fought
The better fight, who single hast maintained

Against revolted multitudes the cause
Of truth, in word mightier than they in arms ;
And for the testimony of truth hast borne
Universal reproach, far worse to bear
Than violence : for this was all thy care,
To stand approved in sight of God, though worlds
Judged thee perverse."

A quartette of colored friends, composed of Mrs. Nellie
B. Mitchell, soprano, Miss Fannie A. Washington, contralto,
Mr. William Walker, tenor, Mr. Lewis A. Fisher, basso,
then sang the following hymn to Handel's "Christmas:" —

"Awake, my soul ! stretch every nerve,
And press with vigor on :
A heavenly race demands thy zeal,
And an immortal crown.

"A cloud of witnesses around
Hold thee in full survey :
Forget the steps already trod,
And onward urge thy way.

"'T is God's all-animating voice
That calls thee from on high ;
'T is his own hand presents the prize
To thine aspiring eye, —

"That prize, with peerless glories bright,
Which shall new lustre boast
When victors' wreaths and monarchs' gems
Shall blend in common dust."

Mr. MAY. — The hymn which has just been sung, as well
as all the others that will be sung on this occasion, were
especial favorites with Mr. Garrison from his youth up,

often sung by him in his family and elsewhere, as so many here know, and they, with others, were the solace and comfort of his sick-chamber, the last night of his consciousness.

REMARKS OF MRS. LUCY STONE.

This day brings us together to aid in the last rites which devolve on those who bury their dead.   One looking from the outside might say, —

> " The sequel of to-day unsolders all
> The goodliest fellowship of famous knights
> Whereof this world holds record.   Such a sleep
> They sleep — the men I loved.   I think that we
> Shall nevermore at any future time
> Delight our souls with talk of knightly deeds.

"But now the whole Round Table is dissolved."

But the personal sorrow and sense of loss which the close of this illustrious life carries to a circle large on both sides of the ocean, almost pass out of sight in the presence of its long record of noblest living.   Instinctively a shout of joy leaps to our lips, as we remember how loyally he stood at his post, three-score years and ten, and how straight his footsteps always followed the clear line of duty.   How in cir-. cumstances of trial, such as rarely fell to mortal lot, his courage never faltered, and his faith never wavered.   With a sublime trust that what is right has the Eternal Forces behind it, and must succeed, he bent every power, without a doubt, and without a fear, to uproot the greatest crime of the age, unmoved by mobs, or by threats, or by entreaties, and he lived to see the triumph of his life-work.   In the thickest of the fight he had always a hand and a word for any other cause that he believed was true : peace, temperance, woman's rights. For this last he stood a tower of strength to its small beginning. To its few solitary workers he said : " You have nothing to fear. No beginning was ever so small and feeble as that of Anti-Slavery. Be hold how the whole nation is stirred on account of it ! "

And if ever there was an hour when those who were moving for the rights of woman needed counsel, we went to him. His knowledge of reform, his cordial interest in the movement itself, made him always our wise and cautious adviser, and to him, I think, the women of this country, like the emancipated slaves, owe, perhaps, more than to any other man. You remember, when the World's Convention at London, in 1840, did not know that women were a part of the world, and would not receive Lucretia Mott, who was sent as one of the delegates from this country, Mr. Garrison went out with her and sat in the gallery. Nothing could induce him to place himself with those who did not recognize the equal rights of all, whether black or white, men or women.

We ought to rejoice that he whose life has just closed has left to us an example grand like the hill-tops against a clear evening sky. It stands out to be a guide and direc-. tion to all of us who come after him. I can think of no funeral in the history of the world where those left behind had so much reason to rejoice. When we look back over his life of more than three-score years and ten, and see it filled with beneficent work, — a work that leaves its mark on this age and on the ages to come, — it seems to me, instead of sorrowing we can rejoice that this example is left us. With the full possession of his powers, this friend has completed his work. We have all read his last letter about the exodus of the colored people from the South. We know

2

it was written amidst paroxysms of pain which stopped his pen ; but it shows the vigor of his intellect and the strength of his purpose were as great as ever. The battle for the freedom of the slaves is fought. To it Mr. Garrison devoted all his best years. But his care for that race ceased only with his life.

For one, in the name of woman, I would express the gratitude which we owe to this man whose hands are cold and still to-day. With what undaunted courage he met the issue, when the question of the rights of woman came into the great movement for which he lived and to which he devoted his best powers! He did not shirk it; he did not dodge it; he did not say, " It does not belong here." He saw that it was a question of human rights, and though it rent the Anti-Slavery Society in twain, and divided its forces for a time, he knew that the Eternal Force was on the side of right, and so he stood with it, and to his courageous defense of it, the wonderful change which has come to the life of woman is largely due. In my heart of hearts I am grateful to him for the great work he did. The veneration of all who appreciate the meaning of the words, " Equal rights for woman," will be paid to his memory forever.

Mr. MAY. — You will now hear from Samuel Johnson.

REMARKS OF REV. SAMUEL JOHNSON.

The silence of this presence, crowded with a love and reverence that have not waited the summons of the body's death, is too full of meaning to be interpreted in words. A voice which has been the unfailing safeguard and succor of righteous purpose for half a century of a nation's struggle for political and moral existence, is forever stilled. When the inevitable event that brings anguish to the nearest and dearest companions plainly comes but to stamp upon the memory of mankind a stainless loyalty to liberty and justice, as leading the way through all the agony of the people's second birth, what room is left for aught but exultant homage to the sweet securities of that providential order in which the life of humanity moves!

This must we emphasize beyond all else : that the movement of principles to universal good can incarnate itself in a personal life with such intensity of truth that the pettiness of individualism is lost in the boundless significance of character. Nothing is so impressive in the closing of the great career on which we look to-day as the sublime warrant of personality it brings to arrest the popular drift to mass-worship and organized mechanism, with their inevitable unbelief in intrinsic values. Its glory centres in having gathered up the moral laws in their whole dealing with this republic, to bear witness past dispute and beyond ignoring, that in their service one is greater than a multitude, the soul master of the state. In these great moments the heaviest private loss is the noblest public education.

It has long seemed clear to me, and I need not say how the conviction deepens in this presence to-day, that to share and represent the imperishableness of principles is the only possible assurance of immortality ; the only evidence it seems worth while to trust. Whoso is part of their path, motive and creative work, may well behold the future as the present, and recognize himself in the life that is to be. Remembering how he lived and moved and had his being in these eternities, what have we to do here with death save as the parting of those outward ties, so dear and so familiar that they cannot vanish but our weak hearts are rent? What have we here to do with death save as the absence from our lawless public strife and perilous drift, of the clear insight, the vigilant heed, the fearless censure, that suffered no delusive compromise in the name of profit, or of peace, to pass without full exposure and reproof? What have we here to do with death save in view of the work yet unaccomplished, beset with duties and dangers uncomprehended as yet; the work awaiting an inexperienced generation, in sore need of those who have the right to warn it in the name of what they have resisted and what they have won? What have we here to do with death, beholding the serene setting of this benignant sun, to rise in the heart of humanity to a day that shall endure so long as men shall remember the sacred liberties of the person, the conscience, and the race, to which all states must do homage and all religions aspire?

For here is one whose conscience was a landmark to his country and his age; voice of the better soul of the republic in its day of degeneracy, summoning it to the task of a self-reformation deemed impossible and absurd, — a task more difficult, because more noble, than the struggle for independence, greater in its significance than any armed victory over foreign or domestic foes. Here is a conscience that never, from the start, would palter with the righteous conditions of success, nor trade away one iota of that integrity which made all sacrifices gain, and knew every compromise to be a loss of power, — a conscience whose unfaltering logic kept its level and held its front against such fallacies and such terrors as these fifty years have hourly bred, — a conscience that pierced straight through an iniquity which had made all organized powers corrupt and blind, to reach and summon a living truth which was its one direct opposite and only cure, — a conscience great enough to comprehend by instinct the identity of that truth with all others that go to make up the dignity of man, to strike the one saving track which included all others, intellectual and spiritual, made possible by the matchless opportunities of the age and the land, and to gather around the movement for which it stood the noblest brotherhood of heart and purpose, in the guardianship of a great constructive idea ; one of those rallying-points for culture, for patriotism, for public virtue, without whose continued inspiration the soul of a nation perishes from the earth.

Above all, here was a conscience greatest in this, that it took its rise in love ; so that in the crowning unity and even identity of these two, his love nourishing his conscience and his conscience illuminating his love, neither could stray from the other, in the central current of his universal work, beset though it was by surface eddies and strifes inseparable from the stress of a revolution ; teeming with possible differences of judgment and conflicts of duty that no man could control and no man fully comprehend.   Pity for the suffering and justice to human nature ; the oppressed to be succored and the moral order to be obeyed to the last tittle ; the soul of the poor to be delivered from the jaws of the spoiler, and the logic of retribution to be enforced that makes men and nations reap as they have sown, — these two sides were with him identical in substance and in force. Their union was the burden of his prophecy, and kept it matched with the broadening interests and demands of the struggle.   From the moment when, almost single-handed, he brought the victim of a blind greed and a blinder piety face to face with his oppressor, amidst the fury of mobs and the contempt of their educators, — and ever since blood and fire, purging every institution and trying every soul, have come to the rescue of duties his little band of heroic men and women had pleaded for in vain, — that divine identity of justice and mercy which he made his own has gone on, step by step, to prove itself the master of the age. And its latest admonition is as impressive as was the first. That toil-spent frame, borne downward to its rest, while the spirit bated not a jot of vision or of love, admonishes us to heed the warning he roused himself from pain and weakness to lift in the hearing of the people, — not to ignore alike their past experience and their present condition in the vanity of trusting only that which they desire to believe.

How vast the band of mourners assembled in our thought around this spirit's unseen transition ! To how very few has it been given in human history to enshrine their obsequies in the blessings of an emancipated race ! And what witnesses to this man's heroic helpfulness, gathered from beyond the seas, from cottage and from court, from masters of men and followers of freedom, from all who lead humanity and all who watch and labor for the coming of its universal religion that shall know no binding creed, no vain superstition, no dividing lines of communion ! Long shall we listen ere we shall fully appreciate the glad tidings of these messengers, beautiful on the mountains of a nation's gratitude, of a world's memory. From that yet unrelieved race in whose service his life was spent, whose feet still stumble in the wilderness, whose hearts quake with the new perils into which our half-policies have brought them, there is yet to come the tribute which only a portion can render now ;

for no coming tribulations, if such must be, will restrain the
natural current of their gratitude to the name of this man,
as one who of his own self-prompted love did for them in
the days of their utter friendlessness a work more worthy of
their homage than any later work of parties, statesmen,
generals, armies or proclamations performed when the justice long refused was extorted from an unwilling people by
forces they could no longer resist. It is but too easy for a
generation conversant only with *political* and *military* dealings with slavery, to disparage the moral protest and perma-
nent educational power of the great abolition movement
which for more than thirty years rocked the foundation of
church and state with its leaven of righteous appeal. But
it will not be so in the days to come. The soul of the people was lifted by that steadfast pressure of an eternal principle, in which the noblest men and women bore their equal
part; though nothing but the thunder of invasion and over-
turn could rouse its *physical* might for the final struggle.
Nor can I grant that this our friend's departure closes an
epoch of national history; that we are passing into another,
with new motives, methods, issues, arguments, and duties.
No great epoch closes with the close of any human eyes in
death. Not by such a figure shall we escape unfinished
tasks; not so suddenly dismiss the still-needed service of
ideas, or of the men who have represented them. The gospel
of the nation's duty and opportunity finds no new inter-
pretation ; the old lessons stand fast, as the old policies and
their perils return. It is the vice of our perfunctory politics
that we expect fresh inspiration before we have learned to
accept and honor what is already given ; that we expect to
advance upon the airy trestle-work of stilted desires instead
of the firm-laid track of duties done.

A nation's growth is by stages where representatives come and go. But principles hold fast on its reluctance till they have shaped it to their law; they forgive no broken promise, suffer no dropped threads in the woof of duty. The great Anti-Slavery message which its ever-hopeful prophet once thought had been heard and heeded, he himself found it his necessity to renew. New men and new occasions succeed the old; but the epoch ends not till its idea is enthroned. No man is omniscient; no man is faultless; no prophet can foretell how the great sin of an age shall be put away; but this cry that it must be put away, and that utterly and speedily, before aught else can prosper, — this will not cease till it is accomplished. What Garrison hoped from the sword of the spirit was found to require the sword of the flesh. But the prophet's limitations must not disparage his truth. Nor let the inevitable conditions on which his great censorship of established beliefs and institutions was lent make men unjust to his spirit, as somewhat that has had its day. Centered in the absolutism of a moral idea which would take no qualification from his desire or will, he could seem severe and strenuous in exacting its claim on the opinions of others. But who that knew him could doubt that tenderness and charity were the tidal wave that floated even his sternest denunciations of individual conduct, still more the emphasis of his argument for personal opinion with valued friends?

I do not forget that we are here to speak to private hearts, to a sense of domestic and personal bereavement that must overflow for the moment even the best appreciation of this public example and incalculable help. What can we do but bring full sheaves of a long-cherished sympathy with your memories of the unfailing light and sweetness that made this large household the seed-ground of high ideals and united desires; the centre of communion for all generous hopes and plans for human weal! With you we recall the simplicity of faith and feeling·that kept its freshness alike in the indignation of a holy war and in the happy play of friendship and domestic life; the inevitable spontaneity that always distinguishes moral genius from the common moralism that is trained by rules. We recall with you that swift and never-failing appreciation which welcomed, as I almost believe, every faithful word that ever, throughout our struggle, fully broke the weak or criminal silence of pulpit and press; that unfaltering trust that suffered no knees to weaken, no heart to flag, in the darkest hour; and we recall with you the tender solicitude with which he guarded your integrity of conviction as his own. Never, surely, has it spoken so sublimely in your hearts as now that it is no longer an outward reliance, but a sure possession, and dear to the maturer love and liberty to which it led your way. And now that ripe integrity of soul has passed to its invisible service in all its fullness, before its fire was dimmed by age, or its rod of power broken, or its clear vision impaired; without one fear or doubt or backward step to mar its unity or enfeeble the sense of its presence and its power. Can you, can we, ask for more than such *euthanasy* to crown the prophet, the father, the friend?

Our fairest households must be scattered; our dearest communion fronts the hour of death; every possession ripens into a renunciation; the tree our ancestors planted outlasts our lifetimes as it did theirs; the pictures that report our likeness seem to be the substance, we the shadows; the longest day allotted for a man to work in is even fleeter now than it was in the unhurried ages when poets could liken it to nothing less swift in flight than the weaver's shuttle. Our bitter partings are the sure surrenders of our best to the friendly bosom of unseen laws into whose depths our own souls hasten to fall. But if what men know of truth, and justice, and beauty, and love, be real, then the truth and justice and love that men *are*, is immortal. For if we know only in part, yet are we of one spirit and one substance with what we know, if our knowing is but life and power. To know and to be known, by participation in that which outlives lifetimes, policies, institutions, and holds men responsible to their best, and to the unity of each with all, is what in all ages has been believed to have conquered death.

Blest is he among men whose ample and adequate task, nobly chosen, greatly loved and greatly achieved, shall live as a reality after him in those whom he loved and gave himself to serve! And most blest among these are they in whose hearts that task and triumph abide, as the dear familiar light of a day that has shone through all their lives. There is no Rock of Ages but the living heart and mind of man!

> " God blesses still the generous thought;
>   And still the fitting word He speeds ;
> And truth at his requiring taught
>   He quickens into deeds.

> " Where is the victory of the grave ?
>   What dust upon the spirit lies ?
> God keeps the sacred life He gave ;
>   The prophet never dies."

I have the honor to read to you a few tribute verses written for this occasion by John G. Whittier : —

GARRISON.

The storm and peril overpast,
  The hounding hatred shamed and still,
Go, soul of freedom! take at last
  The place which thou alone canst fill.

Confirm the lesson taught of old —
  Life saved for self is lost, while they
Who lose it in His service hold
  The lease of God's eternal day.

Not for thyself, but for the slave
  Thy words of thunder shook the world;
No selfish griefs or hatred gave
  The strength wherewith thy bolts were hurled.

From lips that Sinai's trumpet blew
  We heard a tenderer undersong;
Thy very wrath from pity grew,
  From love of man thy hate of wrong.

Now past and present are as one;
  The life below is life above;
Thy mortal years have but begun
  The immortality of love.

With somewhat of thy lofty faith
  We lay thy outworn garment by,
Give death but what belongs to death,
  And life the life that cannot die!

Not for a soul like thine the calm
  Of selfish ease and joys of sense;
But duty, more than crown or palm,
  Its own exceeding recompense.

Go up and on ! thy day well done,
  Its morning promise well fulfilled,
Arise to triumphs yet unwon,
  To holier tasks that God has willed.

Go, leave behind thee all that mars
  The work below of man for man ;
With the white legions of the stars
  Do service such as angels can.

Wherever wrong shall right deny,
  Or suffering spirits urge their plea,
Be thine a voice to smite the lie,
  A hand to set the captive free !

The quartette then sang, to the tune of "Lenox," the
hymn commencing, " Ye tribes of Adam, join : " —

    " Ye tribes of Adam, join
        With heaven and earth and seas,
    And offer notes divine
        To your Creator's praise ;
  Ye holy throng of angels bright,
  In worlds of light begin the song.

    " The shining worlds above
        In glorious order stand,
    Or in swift courses move,
        By his supreme command :
  He spake the word, and all their frame
  From nothing came, to praise the Lord.

    " Let all the nations fear
        The God who rules above ;
    He brings his people near,
        And makes them taste his love :
  While earth and sky attempt his praise,
  His saints shall raise his honors high."

THEODORE D. WELD next addressed the congregation.

REMARKS OF THEODORE D. WELD.

Friends, you have just heard the lines, written perhaps to-day, perhaps yesterday, by our own beloved poet, Whittier. I have in my hand a poem which he wrote almost fifty years ago, in the darkest hour of the midnight which brooded over our country. You are most of you, perhaps all, familiar with it. It is addressed to Mr. Garrison. Shall I read a single stanza? I do it to illustrate a point strongly put by our brother who has just taken his seat; that is, the power of a single soul, *alone*, of a single soul touched with sacred fire, a soul all of whose powers are enlisted, — the thought, the feeling, the susceptibility, the emotion, the indomitable will, the conscience that never shrinks, and always points to duty, — I say, the power which God has lodged in the human mind, enabling it to do and to dare and to suffer everything, and thank God for the privilege of doing it. To show also how, when one soul is thus stirred in its innermost and to its uttermost, it is irresistible; that wherever there are souls, here and there, and thick and fast, too, not merely one, and another, and another, of the great mass, but multitudes of souls are ready to receive the truth and welcome it, to incorporate it into their thought and feeling, to live and die for it. That was the effect of Garrison upon the soul of Whittier. He here gives us his testimony. The date of this is 1833, — almost fifty years ago. He says in the third stanza, —

> "I love thee with a brother's love,
> I feel my pulses thrill
> To mark thy spirit soar above
> The cloud of human ill.

My heart hath leaped to answer thine,
    And echo back thy words,
As leaps the warrior's at the shine
    And flash of kindred swords !"

Friends, in recounting the multiform cords upon which
our great brother struck, and in following out those vibra-
tions until we see them rouse the nation's heart, — in doing
this we come to a point where we stand amazed beyond
our belief; we have seen nothing like it; we have thought
of nothing like it; we know of nothing like it in the history of the world; where, on moral grounds, through the
dictate of conscience, through the grasp of the intuitions,
such force has been given to a single soul as to make it
omnipotent. No wonder that the old prophet broke out, " I
said, Ye are gods!" When God pulsates in a human soul,
God is there. Not the Infinite God, the eternal existence,
but the power of God; that which Jesus felt when He said,
" To this end was I born, and for this cause came I into the
world, to bear witness unto the truth ; " and " the words I
speak unto you, they are spirit and they are life." Think for
a moment of Garrison, through his paper and by his speech,
traversing the country, uttering words which fell with such
force as to break the spell that was upon souls, rouse the
latent and dormant and bring them to life, gird them with
power, and put weapons into their hands, arming them from
head to foot, to go forth and fight in the moral warfare!

It has been said by those who have preceded me, that
we are not here to mourn. In looking over this congregation, I do not see a single face that seems to mourn. It is
no hour for mourning. Why should we mourn here when
they are exulting *there ?* When they are receiving him
with greetings and with songs of joy upon their lips, and

putting the crown upon his head! "Well-dones" and
"Welcomes" are echoing there: why should be wailing
here? We cannot wail. We are here to rejoice. We
are here to make this a solemn and glorious festival of the
spirit. We are here to thank God and take courage that
such a man has lived. In devout gratitude we bow before
Him, saying: "Blessing, and honor, and glory, and thanksgiving to Him that sitteth upon the throne, that He hath
given us, given this nation, given the world, so precious a
thing as a human soul such as animated that form which
lies motionless there."

Let us rejoice! Tears will come to our eyes, but they
are not tears of bereavement. If we have grief, it is the
joy of grief. They are tears of love; they are tears of
sympathy; they are tears of exultation. Blessed are we
that we have lived at the same time when there walked the
earth such a man as WILLIAM LLOYD GARRISON. We did
not know him. Those that knew him best did not know
his innermost and his uttermost. The world around did
not know him, even those who most appreciated him. Fifty
years hence there will be something written about Garrison
that will show what no one has exhibited or can exhibit
now, for then time enough will have elapsed for his influence, the power of his soul, for those vast pulsations, so far-
reaching, — time enough to trace out all those lines of influence and show how they stamped hearts innumerable, and
how they can be traced in vast and manifold effects. Great
as the direct influence of the life of Garrison was, great as
it is to the multitudes of the freedmen of the South who
rise up to testify, great as is the direct influence which out-
poured from his life, the indirect influences seem almost
greater. He saw, at one of the main points of the human

circle, something which compelled his attention, something
which could not be ignored, which should not be left any
longer ; and he lifted up his voice and cried out against it,
beseeched, appealed, and summoned up help from every
quarter, and touched with such force as no man else could
the springs that could accomplish his object, — the abolition
of slavery.

But that was only one point in the great circle of human
interests, human rights, and human well-being. Now, indi-
rectly, this line being traversed as he traversed it, — all the
light thrown upon rights that he threw, — why, it led to
other points of the circle ; and then, as has been alluded to
by our sister here, in considering the question of rights, what
they are, it was seen that self-right is the foundation of all
right, the nucleus, the centre, from which all other rights
radiate ; that it is really the trunk of the tree of all rights,
and that every other right is a mere relative right to self-
right, in the centre ; and that the great heart that animates
that right in the centre is *myself*. Take away the right to
myself, and where is my right to my coat, or my book, or
my anything else ? It is nothing ; it is uprooted and cast
away to wither ! He brought his mind to a focus upon the
fundamental right, the intrinsic, the absolute, the eternal,
the ineradicable right — *self-right*. And that was the reason why he uttered what are called such hard words about
slaveholding. It was the same conviction that fired the
soul of old John Wesley, — blessings on him ! — when he
said, " Slavery is the sum of all villanies ! " No wonder he
used words that sounded hard to those very soft and shrink-
ing people who loved smooth things, and to those who sym-
pathized with slavery. Why, when he saw the slaveholder
not merely asserting his right to a man as a piece of prop-

erty, but when he saw him stalking over all this New England and claiming the right to absorb into himself the self-
right of another self and call it his, make it an article of
property, and send it to the auction-block, no wonder, he
roused at length the North, no wonder the slaveholders
put a price upon his head, because there he touched the
apple of their eye. He had struck the very heart of the
monster. It was a death-blow, and that must be fended off,
or all must be given up.

Friends, you have been detained long already. I ought
not to keep you from those words to which you are waiting
to listen, from our brother who, more than any one else,
struck blows and uttered words such as no other could ex-
cept the great leader, — uttered words, gave a testimony,
and stamped an impression upon the nation's heart. You
want to hear him, and not to hear me. But let me ask
your patience for a moment longer. Some have said, we are
not here to eulogize our brother. It really seems as though
words were very weak in eulogy of WILLIAM LLOYD
GARRISON. The truth is, we are shut up to the necessity
of praising him. We cannot speak his name but it is the
highest praise that can be given him. Who does not recognize that? Who can speak of a single one of his acts without that act rising up and testifying to what he was, to
what he is, to what he has done, and what no other man
did or could do? No, it is all around, from centre to circum-
ference alike! See how the whole land is strewn with his
deeds! See how the very air breathes of them! See how
the very tones of the wind, as they go through the forest,
shout them! The fact is, nothing that he has done can be
spoken of that is not a eulogy. And yet, if those cold lips
could move and utter words, it seems to me they would say,

3

"In this hour let eulogy be dumb!" Blessed brother! we would let eulogy be dumb, if it were possible. But then we must stand dumb ourselves. We can say nothing at such a time as this if we cannot speak of what he has done, and every act is a eulogy. Why, those words that were repeated by our brother who has addressed you, — what marvelous words they were! Marvelous they will be forever.

Let us for a moment look back fifty years. We see a church dead! Not merely blind and palsied, but *dead* to the sin of slavery. Whatever life it had, there was no pulsation indicating that it realized the sin of slavery. Look back there! What do we see? A great bank of darkness, in which the church lies dead; and as we look, we see a single hand unshrinkingly thrust out from the thickest of that darkness and writing a dozen simple words, little fireside words; writing them so large that they can be seen and read from far. We see those words take on a glow in the midst of the very darkness. We see those letters every one turned to a letter of fire. And what was written there? You have heard them already; you know them by heart: "*I am in earnest. I will not equivocate — I will not excuse — I will not retreat a single inch —* AND I WILL BE HEARD!" Take the circumstances and conditions of the time in which they were uttered, consider the great soul that propelled them forth, consider that he felt the necessity upon him and a woe unto him if he did not utter them, — consider all this, and then tell me whether such words have ever been uttered by other mortal lips! Those words were the passwords of Liberty. They were the keynote, struck by him so loud that they startled the nation. Thank God that there was one man in those times who could utter them; who had a soul large enough, deep enough, strong enough, fired enough, godlike enough, to utter them!

The quartette then sang the following hymn, the congregation spontaneously rising and joining in singing the familiar words, to the tune of " Amsterdam : " —

" Rise, my soul! and stretch thy wings, —
    Thy better portion trace ;
Rise, from transitory things,
    Towards heaven, thy native place.
Sun and moon and stars decay,
    Time shall soon this earth remove ;
Rise, my soul ! and haste away
    To seats prepared above.

" Rivers to the ocean run,
    Nor stay in all their course ;
Fire ascending seeks the sun, —
    Both speed them to their source :
So a soul that's born of God
    Pants to view his glorious face,
Upward tends to his abode,
    To rest in his embrace."

REMARKS OF WENDELL PHILLIPS.

It has been well said that we are not here to weep, and neither are we here to praise. No life closes without sadness. Death, after all, no matter what hope or what memories surround it, is terrible and a mystery. We never part hands that have been clasped life-long in loving tenderness but the hour is sad ; still, we do not come here to weep. In other moments, elsewhere, we can offer tender and loving sympathy to those whose roof-tree is so sadly bereaved. But in the spirit of the great life which we commemorate, this hour is for the utterance of a lesson ; this hour is given to contemplate a grand example, a rich inheritance, a noble life worthily ended. You come together, not to pay tribute, even loving tribute, to the friend you have lost, whose features you will miss from daily life, but to remember the grand lesson of that career; to speak to each other and to emphasize what that life teaches, — especially in the hearing of these young listeners, who did not see that marvelous career; in their hearing to construe the meaning of the great name which is borne world-wide, and tell them why on both sides the ocean, the news of his death is a matter of interest to every lover of his race. As my friend said, we have no right to be silent. Those of us who stood near him, who witnessed the secret springs of his action, the consistent inward and outward life, have no right to be silent. The largest contribution that will ever be made by any single man's life to the knowledge of the working of our institutions will be the picture of his career. He sounded the depths of the weakness, he proved the ultimate strength, of republican institutions; he gave us to know the perils that confront us; he taught us to rally the strength that lies hid.

To my mind there are three remarkable elements in his career. One is rare even among great men. It was his own moral nature, unaided, uninfluenced from outside, that consecrated him to a great idea. Other men ripen gradually. The youngest of the great American names that will be compared with his was between thirty and forty when his first anti-slavery word was uttered. Luther was thirty-four years old when an infamous enterprise woke him to indignation, and it then took two years more to reveal to him the mission God designed for him. This man was in jail for his opinions when he was just twenty-four. He had confronted a nation in the very bloom of his youth. It could be said of him more than of any other American in our day, and more than of any great leader that I chance now to remember in any epoch, that he did not need circumstances, outside influence, some great pregnant event to press him into service, to provoke him to thought, to kindle him into enthusiasm. His moral nature was as marvelous as was the intellect of Pascal. It seemed to be born fully equipped, "finely touched." Think of the mere dates; think that at some twenty-four years old, while Christianity and statesmanship, the experience, the genius of the land, were wandering in the desert, aghast, amazed, and confounded over a frightful evil, a great sin, this boy sounded, found, invented the talisman, "Immediate, unconditional emancipation on the soil." You may say he borrowed it — true enough — from the lips of a woman on the other side of the Atlantic, but he was the only American whose moral nature seemed, just on the edge of life, so perfectly open to duty and truth that it answered to the far-off bugle-note, and proclaimed it instantly as a complete solution of the problem.

Young men, you have no conception of the miracle of that insight; for it is not given to you to remember with any vividness the blackness of the darkness of ignorance and indifference which then brooded over what was called the moral and religious element of the American people. When I think of him, as Melancthon said of Luther, "day by day grows the wonder fresh" at the ripeness of the moral and intellectual life that God gave him at the very opening.

You hear that boy's lips announcing the statesmanlike solution which startled politicians and angered church and

people. A year afterwards, with equally single-hearted
devotion, in words that have been so often quoted, with
those dungeon doors behind him, he enters on his career.
In January, 1831, then twenty-five years old, he starts the
publication of the " Liberator," advocating the immediate
abolition of slavery ; and, with the sublime pledge, " I will
be as harsh as truth and as uncompromising as justice. On
this subject I do not wish to speak or write with modera-
tion. I will not equivocate — I will not excuse — I will not
retreat a single inch — AND I WILL BE HEARD."

Then began an agitation which for the marvel of its
origin, the majesty of its purpose, the earnestness, unselfishness and ability of its appeals, the vigor of its assault,
the deep national convulsion it caused, the vast and beneficent changes it wrought, and its wide-spread, indirect influence on all kindred moral questions, is without a parallel
in history since Luther. This boy created and marshaled
it. His converts held it up and carried it on. Before this,
all through the preceding century, there had been among
us scattered and single abolitionists, earnest and able men ;
sometimes, like Wythe of Virginia, in high places. The
Quakers and Covenanters had never intermitted their testimony against slavery. But Garrison was the first man to
begin a *movement* designed to annihilate slavery. He an-
nounced the principle, arranged the method, gathered the
forces, enkindled the zeal, started the argument, and finally
marshaled the nation for and against .the system in a conflict that came near rending the Union.

I marvel again at the instinctive sagacity which discerned
the hidden forces fit for such a movement, called them forth,
and wielded them to such prompt results. Archimedes said,
" Give me a spot and I will move the world." O'Connell

leaned back on three millions of Irishmen, all on fire with sympathy. Cobden's hands were held up by the whole manufacturing interest of Great Britain; his treasury was the wealth of the middle classes of the country, and behind him also, in fair proportion, stood the religious convictions of England. Marvelous was their agitation; as you gaze upon it in its successive stages and analyze it, you are astonished at what they invented for tools. But this boy stood alone; utterly alone, at first. There was no sympathy anywhere; his hands were empty; one single penniless comrade was his only helper. Starving on bread and water, he could command the use of types, that was all. Trade endeavored to crush him; the intellectual life of America disowned him.

My friend Weld has said the church was a thick bank of black cloud looming over him. Yes. But no sooner did the church discern the impetuous boy's purpose than out of that dead, sluggish cloud thundered and lightened a malignity which could not find words to express its hate. The very pulpit where I stand saw this apostle of liberty and justice sore beset, always in great need, and often in deadly peril; yet it never gave him one word of approval or sympathy. During all his weary struggle, Mr. Garrison felt its weight in the scale against him. In those years it led the sect which arrogates to itself the name of Liberal. If this was the bearing of so-called Liberals, what bitterness of opposition, judge ye, did not the others show? A mere boy confronts church, commerce, and college; a boy, with neither training nor experience! Almost at once the assault tells; the whole country is hotly interested. What created such life under those ribs of death? Whence came that instinctive knowledge? Where did he get that sound

common sense? Whence did he summon that almost un-
erring sagacity which, starting agitation on an untried field,
never committed an error, provoking year by year addi-
tional enthusiasm ; gathering, as he advanced, helper after
helper to his side! I marvel at the miraculous boy. He
had no means. Where he got, whence he summoned, how
he created, the elements which changed 1830 into 1835
—1830 apathy, indifference, ignorance, icebergs, into 1835,
every man intelligently hating him, and mobs assaulting
him in every city — is a marvel which none but older men
than I can adequately analyze and explain. He said to a
friend who remonstrated with him on the heat and severity
of his language, " Brother, I have need to be all on fire, for
I have mountains of ice about me to melt." Well, that
dungeon of 1830, that universal apathy, that deadness of
soul, that contempt of what called itself intellect, in ten
years he changed into the whole country aflame. He made
every single home, press, pulpit, and senate-chamber a de-
bating society, with *his* right and wrong for the subject.
And as was said of Luther, " God honored him by making
all the worst men his enemies."

Fastened on that daily life was a malignant attention and
criticism such as no American has ever endured. I will
not call it a criticism of hate ; that word is not strong
enough. Malignity searched him with candles from the
moment he uttered that God-given solution of the problem to the moment when he took the hand of the nation
and wrote out the statute which made it law. Malignity
searched those forty years with candles, and yet even malignity has never lisped a suspicion, much less a charge —
never lisped a suspicion of anything mean, dishonorable,
dishonest. No man, however mad with hate, however fierce

in assault, ever dared to hint that there was anything low in motive, false in assertion, selfish in purpose, dishonest in method — never a stain on the thought, the word, or the deed.

Now contemplate this boy entering such an arena, confronting a nation and all its forces, utterly poor, with no sympathy from any quarter, conducting an angry, widespread, and profound agitation for ten, twenty, forty years, amid the hate of everything strong in American life, and the contempt of everything influential, and no stain, not the slightest shadow of one, rests on his escutcheon ! Summon me the public men, the men who have put their hands to the helm of the vessel of state since 1789, of whom that can be said, although love and admiration, which almost culminated in worship, attended the steps of some of them.

Then look at the work he did. My friends have spoken of his influence. What American ever held his hand so long and so powerfully on the helm of social, intellectual, and moral America ? There have been giants in our day. Great men God has granted in widely different spheres; earnest men, men whom public admiration lifted early into power. I shall venture to name some of them. Perhaps you will say it is not usual on an occasion like this, but long-waiting truth needs to be uttered in an hour when this great example is still absolutely indispensable to inspire the effort, to guide the steps, to cheer the hope, of the nation not yet arrived in the promised land. I want to show you the vast breadth and depth that this man's name signifies. We have had Webster in the Senate ; we have had Lyman Beecher in the pulpit ; we have had Calhoun at the head of a section ; we have had a philosopher at Concord with his inspiration penetrating the young mind of the

Northern States. They are the four men that history, perhaps, will mention somewhere near the great force whose
closing in this scene we commemorate to-day. Remember
now not merely the inadequate means at this man's control, not simply the bitter hate that he confronted, not the
vast work that he must be allowed to have done, — surely
vast, when measured by the opposition he encountered and
the strength he held in his hands, — but dismissing all those
considerations, measuring nothing but the breadth and depth
of his hold, his grasp on American character, social change,
and general progress, what man's signet has been set so deep,
planted so forever on the thoughts of his epoch? Trace
home intelligently, trace home to their sources, the changes
social, political, intellectual and religious, that have come
over us during the last fifty years, — the volcanic convulsions,
the stormy waves which have tossed and rocked our generation, — and you will find close at the sources of the Mississippi this boy with his proclamation!

The great party that put on record the statute of freedom
was made up of men whose conscience he quickened and
whose intellect he inspired, and they long stood the tools of
a public opinion that he created. The grandest name beside his in the America of our times is that of John Brown.
Brown stood on the platform that Garrison built; and Mrs.
Stowe herself charmed an audience that he gathered for
her, with words which he inspired, from a heart that he
kindled. Sitting at his feet were leaders born of the " Liberator," the guides of public sentiment. I know whereof I
affirm. It was often a pleasant boast of Charles Sumner
that he read the " Liberator " two years before I did, and
among the great men who followed his lead and held up his
hands in Massachusetts, where is the intellect, where is the

heart that does not trace to this printer boy the first pulse that bade him serve the slave? For myself, no words can adequately tell the measureless debt I owe him, the moral and intellectual life he opened to me. I feel like the old Greek, who, taught himself by Socrates, called his own scholars " the disciples of Socrates."

This is only another instance added to the roll of the Washingtons and the Hampdens, whose root is not ability, but *character;* that influence which, like the great Master's of Judea (humanly speaking), spreading through the centuries, testifies that the world suffers its grandest changes not by genius, but by the more potent control of *character.* His was an earnestness that would take no denial, that consumed opposition in the intensity of its convictions, that knew nothing but right. As friend after friend gathered slowly, one by one, to his side, in that very meeting of a dozen heroic men, to form the New England Anti-Slavery Society, it was his compelling hand, his resolute unwillingness to temper or qualify the utterance, that finally dedicated that first organized movement to the doctrine of immediate emancipation. He seems to have understood — this boy without experience — he seems to have understood by instinct that righteousness is the only thing which will finally compel submission; that one, with God, is always a majority. He seems to have known it at the very outset, taught of God, the herald and champion, God-endowed and God-sent to arouse a nation, that only by the most absolute assertion of the uttermost truth, without qualification or compromise, can a nation be waked to conscience or strengthened for duty. No man ever understood so thoroughly — not O'Connell, nor Cobden — the nature and needs of that *agitation* which alone, in our day, reforms states. In the

darkest hour he never doubted the omnipotence of conscience
and the moral sentiment.

And then look at the unquailing courage with which he
faced the successive obstacles that confronted him! Modest,
believing at the outset that America could not be as corrupt as she seemed, he waits at the door of the churches,
importunes leading clergymen, begs for a voice from the
sanctuary, a consecrated protest from the pulpit. To his
utter amazement, he learns, by thus probing it, that the
church will give him no help, but, on the contrary, surges
into the movement in opposition. Serene, though astounded
by the unexpected revelation, he simply turns his footsteps,
and announces that " a Christianity which keeps peace
with the oppressor is no Christianity," and goes on his way
to supplant the religious element which the church had
allied with sin by a deeper religious faith. Yes, he sets
himself to work, this stripling with his sling confronting the
angry giant in complete steel, this solitary evangelist, to
make Christians of twenty millions of people! I am not ex-
aggerating. You know, older men, who can go back to that
period ; I know that when one, kindred to a voice that you
have heard to-day, whose pathway Garrison's bloody feet
had made easier for the treading, when he uttered in a pulpit in Boston only a few strong words, injected in the course
of a sermon, his venerable father, between seventy and
eighty years, was met the next morning and his hand
shaken by a much moved friend. " Colonel, you have my
sympathy. I cannot tell you how much I pity you."
" What," said the brusque old man, " what is your pity ? "
" Well, I hear your son went crazy at ' Church Green '
yesterday." Such was the utter indifference. At that time,
bloody feet had smoothed the pathway for other men to

tread. Still, then and for years afterwards, insanity was
the only kind-hearted excuse that partial friends could find
for sympathy with such a madman!
If anything strikes one more prominently than another in
this career — to your astonishment, young men, you may say
— it is the plain, sober common sense, the robust English
element which underlay Cromwell, which explains Hamp-
den, which gives the color that distinguishes 1640 in England from 1790 in France. Plain, robust, well-balanced
common sense. Nothing erratic; no enthusiasm which had
lost its hold on firm earth; no mistake of method; no
unmeasured confidence; no miscalculation of the enemy's
strength. Whoever mistook, Garrison seldom mistook.
Fewer mistakes in that long agitation of fifty years can be
charged to his account than to any other American. Erratic
as men supposed him, intemperate in utterance, mad in judgment, an enthusiast gone crazy, the moment you sat down
at his side, patient in explanation, clear in statement, sound
in judgment, studying carefully every step, calculating every
assault, measuring the force to meet it, never in haste, always patient, waiting until the time ripened, — fit for a
great leader. Cull, if you please, from the statesmen who
obeyed him, whom he either whipped into submission or
summoned into existence, cull from among them the man
whose career, fairly examined, exhibits fewer miscalcula-
tions and fewer mistakes than this career which is just
ended.

I know what I claim. As Mr. Weld has said, I am
speaking to-day to men who judge by their ears, by rumors;
who see, not with their eyes, but with their prejudices. History, fifty years hence, dispelling your prejudices, will do
justice to the grand sweep of the orbit which, as my friend

said, to-day we are hardly in a position, or mood, to meas-
ure.   As Coleridge avers, " The truth-haters of to-morrow
will give the right name to the truth haters of to-day, for
even such men the stream of time bears onward." I do not
fear that if my words are remembered by the next generation they will be thought unsupported or extravagant.
When history seeks the sources of New England character,
when men begin to open up and examine the hidden springs
and note the convulsions and the throes of American life
within the last half century, they will remember Parker,
that Jupiter of the pulpit ; they will remember the long
unheeded but measureless influence that came to us from
the seclusion of Concord ; they will do justice to the mas-
terly statesmanship which guided, during a part of his life,
the efforts of Webster, but they will recognize that there
was only one man north of Mason and Dixon's line who
met squarely, with an absolute logic, the else impregnable
position of John C. Calhoun ; only one brave, far-sighted,
keen, logical intellect, which discerned that there were only
two moral points in the universe, *right* and *wrong ;* that
when one was asserted, subterfuge and evasion would be
sure to end in defeat.

Here lie the brain and the heart ; here lies the statesmanlike intellect, logical as Jonathan Edwards, brave as Luther, which confronted the logic of South Carolina with an
assertion direct and broad enough to make an issue and
necessitate a conflict of two civilizations. Calhoun said,
Slavery is *right.* Webster and Clay shrunk from him and
evaded his assertion. Garrison, alone at that time, met
him face to face, proclaiming slavery a sin and daring all
the inferences.   It is true, as New Orleans complains to-day
in her journals, that this man brought upon America every-

thing they call the disaster of the last twenty years; and it is equally true that if you seek through the hidden causes and unheeded events for the hand that wrote "emancipation" on the statute-book and on the flag, it lies still there to-day.

I have no time to number the many kindred reforms to which he lent as profound an earnestness and almost as large aid.

I hardly dare enter that home. There is one other marked, and, as it seems to me, unprecedented, element in this career. His was the happiest life I ever saw. No need for pity. Let no tear fall over his life. No man gathered into his bosom a fuller sheaf of blessing, delight, and joy. In his seventy years, there were not arrows enough in the whole quiver of the church or state to wound him. As Guizot once said from the tribune, "Gentlemen, you cannot get high enough to reach the level of my contempt." So Garrison, from the serene level of his daily life, from the faith that never faltered, was able to say to American hate, "You cannot reach up to the level of my home mood, my daily existence." I have seen him intimately for thirty years, while raining on his head was the hate of the community, when by every possible form of expression malignity let him know that it wished him all sorts of harm. I never saw him unhappy; I never saw the moment that serene, abounding faith in the rectitude of his motive, the soundness of his method, and the certainty of his success did not lift him above all possibility of being reached by any clamor about him. Every one of his near friends will agree with me that this was the happiest life God has granted in our day to any American standing in the foremost rank of influence and effort.

Adjourned from the stormiest meeting, where hot debate had roused all his powers as near to anger as his nature ever let him come, the music of a dozen voices — even of those who had just opposed him — or a piano, if the house held one, changed his mood in an instant, and made the hour laugh with more than content; unless indeed, a baby and playing with it proved metal even more attractive.

To champion wearisome causes, bear with disordered intellects, to shelter the wrecks of intemperance and fugitives whose pulse trembled at every touch on the door-latch — this was his home; keenly alive to human suffering, ever prompt to help relieve it, pouring out his means for that more lavishly than he ought — all this was no burden, never clouded or depressed the inextinguishable buoyancy and gladness of his nature. God ever held over him unclouded the sunlight of his countenance.

And he never grew old. The tabernacle of flesh grew feebler and the step was less elastic. But the ability to work, the serene faith and unflagging hope suffered no change. To the day of his death he was as ready as in his boyhood to confront and defy a mad majority. The keen insight and clear judgment never failed him. His tenacity of purpose never weakened. He showed nothing either of the intellectual sluggishness or the timidity of age. The bugle-call which, last year, woke the nation to its peril and duty on the Southern question, showed all the old fitness to lead and mould a people's course. Younger men might be confused or dazed by plausible pretensions, and half the North was befooled; but the old pioneer detected the false ring as quickly as in his youth. The words his dying hand traced, welcoming the Southern exodus and foretelling its result, had all the defiant courage and prophetic solemnity of his youngest and boldest days.

Serene, fearless, marvelous man! Mortal, with so few shortcomings!

Farewell, for a very little while, noblest of Christian men! Leader, brave, tireless, unselfish! When the ear heard thee, then it blessed thee ; the eye that saw thee gave witness to thee. More truly than it could ever heretofore be said since the great patriarch wrote it, " the blessing of him that was ready to perish " was thine eternal great reward.

Though the clouds rest for a moment to-day on the great work that you set your heart to accomplish, you knew, God in his love let you see, that your work was done ; that one thing, by his blessing on your efforts, is fixed beyond the possibility of change. While that ear could listen, God gave what He has so rarely given to man, the plaudits and prayers of four millions of victims, thanking you for emancipation, and through the clouds of to-day your heart, as it ceased to beat, felt certain, *certain*, that whether one flag or two shall rule this continent in time to come, one thing is settled — it never henceforth can be trodden by a slave!

Mr. MAY. — A word should properly be said in acknowledgment of the great courtesy which has granted to the family and the friends of Mr. Garrison in this large audience the use of this spacious house. We all recognize the courtesy, and offer our thanks.

I am desired to say that those in this audience who would like to look once more upon what remains of WILLIAM LLOYD GARRISON will have now an opportunity to do so.

Almost the entire congregation availed themselves of this privilege, and then the body was taken from the church to

4

Forest Hills Cemetery, where, as the last rays of the setting sun rested upon this beautiful " city of the dead," and glorified the spot, with tender and reverent hands it was laid in the grave, in the presence of his children and grandchildren, and very many of his old associates in the struggle for freedom. The services were fitly closed by the singing of the hymn commencing: " I cannot always trace the way," by the friends who had rendered such acceptable service at the church, and all that was mortal of WILLIAM LLOYD GARRISON was left to its rest.

THE DAY OF SMALL THINGS.

BY JAMES RUSSELL LOWELL.

"Some time afterward, it was reported to me by the city officers that they had ferreted out the paper and its editor. His office was an obscure hole; his only visible auxiliary a negro boy; and his supporters a few very insignificant persons, of all colors." — *Letter of Hon. H. G. Otis.*

In a small chamber, friendless and unseen,
    Toiled o'er his types one poor, unlearned young man;
The place was dark, unfurnitured and mean,
    Yet there the freedom of a race began.

Help came but slowly; surely, no man yet
    Put lever to the heavy world with less;
What need of help? He knew how types were set,
    He had a dauntless spirit and a press.

Such earnest natures are the fiery pith,
    The compact nucleus round which systems grow;
Mass after mass becomes inspired therewith,
    And whirls impregnate with the central glow.

O Truth! O Freedom! how are ye still born
    In the rude stable, in the manger nursed!
What humble hands unbar those gates of morn
    Through which the splendors of the New Day burst!

What! shall one monk, scarce known beyond his cell,
    Front Rome's far-reaching bolts, and scorn her frown?
Brave Luther answered, YES! — that thunder's swell
    Rocked Europe, and discharmed the triple crown.

" Whatever can be known of Earth we know,"
    Sneered Europe's wise men, in their snail-shells curled ;
No ! said one man in Genoa ; and that No
    Out of the dark created this New World.

Who is it will not dare himself to trust?
    Who is it hath not strength to stand alone?
Who is it thwarts and bilks the inward MUST ?
    He and his works like sand from earth are blown.

Men of a thousand shifts and wiles, look here !
    See one straightforward conscience put in pawn
To win a world !   See the obedient sphere,
    By bravery's simple gravitation drawn !

Shall we not heed the lesson taught of old,
    And by the Present's lips repeated still,
In our own single manhood to be bold,
    Fortressed in conscience and impregnable will ?

We stride the river daily at its spring,
    Nor in our childish thoughtlessness foresee
What myriad vassal streams shall tribute bring,
    How like an equal it shall greet the sea.

O small beginnings, ye are great and strong,
    Based on a faithful heart and weariless brain ;
Ye build the future fair, ye conquer wrong,
    Ye earn the crown, and wear it not in vain !

APPENDIX.

HELEN ELIZA BENSON,

Wife of William Lloyd Garrison.

[As this volume will be read by many who have never seen the Memorial volume to Mrs. Garrison, prepared by her husband after her death, in 1876, for private distribution among friends, it is deemed fitting that the following tribute to her character, in the remarks of Wendell Phillips at her funeral, should be included in these pages.]

REMARKS OF WENDELL PHILLIPS.

How hard it is to let our friends go! We cling to them as if separation were separation forever; and yet, as life nears its end, and we tread the last years together, have we any right to be surprised that the circle grows narrow? — that so many fall, one after another, at our side? Death seems to strike very frequently ; but it is only the natural, inevitable fate, however sad for the moment.

Some of us can recollect, only twenty years ago, the large and loving group that lived and worked together; the joy of companionship, sympathy with each other — almost our only joy — for the outlook was very dark, and our toil seemed almost vain. The world's dislike of what we aimed at, the social frown, obliged us to be all the world to each other; and yet it was a full life. The life was worth living; the labor was its own reward ; we lacked nothing.

As I stand by this dust, my thoughts go freshly back to those pleasant years when the warp and woof of her life were woven so close to the rest of us ; when the sight of it was such an inspiration. How cheerfully she took up daily the burden of sacrifice and effort! With what serene courage she looked into the face of peril to her own life, and to those who were dearer to her than life ! A young bride brought under such dark skies, and so ready for them. Trained among Friends, with the blood of martyrdom and self-sacrifice in her veins, she came so naturally to the altar! And when the gallows was erected in front of the young bride's windows, never from that stout soul did the husband get look or word that bade him do anything but go steadily forward, and take no counsel of

man. Sheltered in the jail, a great city hunting for his life, how
strong he must have been when they brought him his young wife's
brave words: "I know my husband will never betray his principles!" Helpmeet, indeed, for the pioneer in that terrible fight.
The most unselfish of human beings, she poured all her strength
into the lives of those about her, without asking acknowledgment
or recognition, unconscious of the sacrifice. With marvelous ability, what would have been weary burdens to others, she lifted so
gayly! A young mother, with the cares of a growing family, not
rich in means, only her own hands to help, yet never failing in
cheerful welcome to every call ; doing for others as if her life was
all leisure and her hands full. With rare executive ability, doing
a great deal, and so easily as to never seem burdened! Who ever
saw her reluct at any sacrifice her own purpose or her husband's
made necessary? No matter how long and weary the absence, no
matter how lonely he left her, she cheered and strengthened him to
the sacrifice if his great cause asked it. The fair current of her
husband's grand purpose swept on unchecked by any distracting
anxiety. Her energy and unselfishness left him all his strength free
for the world's service.

Many of you have seen her only in years when illness hindered
her power. You can hardly appreciate the large help she gave the
Anti-Slavery movement.

That home was a great help. Her husband's word and pen
scattered his purpose far and wide; but the comrades that his ideas
brought to his side her welcome melted into friends. No matter
how various and discordant they were in many things — no matter
how much there was to bear and overlook — her patience and her
thanks for their sympathy in the great idea were always sufficient
for this work also. She made a family of them, and her roof was
always a home for all. And who shall say how much that served
the great cause? Yet drudgery did not choke thought ; care never
narrowed her interest. She was not merely the mother, or the
head of a home; her own life and her husband's moved hand in
hand in such loving accord, seemed so exactly one, that it was
hard to divide their work. At the fireside, — in the hours, not fre-

quent, of relaxation, — in scenes of stormy debate, — that beautiful presence, of rare sweetness and dignity, what an inspiration and power it was! And then the mother — fond, painstaking, faithful! No mother who bars every generous thought out from her life, and in severe seclusion forgets everything but her children — no such mother was ever more exact in every duty, ready for every care, faithful at every point, more lavish in fond thoughtfulness, than this mother, whose cares never narrowed the broad idea of life she brought from her girlhood's home.

Who can forget her modest dignity — shrinkingly modest — yet ever equal to the high place events called her to? In that group of remarkable men and women which the Anti-Slavery movement drew together, she had her own niche, — which no one else could have filled so perfectly or unconsciously as she did. And in that rounded life no over-zeal in one channel, no extra service at one point, need be offered as excuse for shortcoming elsewhere. She forgot, omitted nothing. How much we all owe her! She is not dead. She has gone before; but she has not gone away. Nearer than ever, this very hour she watches and ministers to those in whose lives she was so wrapped; to whose happiness she was so devoted. Who thinks that loving heart could be happy if it were not allowed to minister to those she loved? How easy it is to fancy the welcome the old faces have given her! The honored faces; the familiar faces; the old tones, that have carried her back to the pleasant years of health, and strength, and willing labor! How gladly she broke the bonds that hindered her activity! There are more there than here. Very slight the change seems to her! She has not left us, — she has rejoined them. She has joined the old band that worked life-long for the true and the good. The dear, familiar names, how freshly they come to our lips! We can see them bend over and lift her up to them, to a broader life. Faith is sight to-day. She works on a higher level; ministers to old ideas; guards lovingly those she went through life with. Even in that higher work they watch for our coming also. Let the years yet spared us here be warning to make ourselves fit for that companionship!

The separation is hard. Nature will have its way. " The heart knoweth its own bitterness," and for a while loves to dwell on it; needs perhaps to dwell on it. But the hour is just here, knocking at the door, when we shall thank God not only for the long years of companionship, and health, and example, which she has given us, but for this great relief: that, in fullness of time, in loving-kindness, He hath broken the bond which hindered her. No heaven that is not a home to her. She worked with God here, and He has taken her into his nearer presence. We are sad because of the void at our side. It is hard to have the path so empty around us. We miss that face and those tones But that is the body: limited, narrow, of little faith. The soul shines through in a moment, sees its own destiny, and thanks God for the joyous change We draw sad breaths now. We miss the magnet that kept this home together. We miss the tie that lovingly bound so many lives into one life. That is broken. We peer into the future and fear for another void still, and a narrower circle, not knowing which of us will be taken next. With an effort of patience — with half-submission — we bow to God's dealings. That is only for an hour. In a little while we shall remember the grand life ; we shall thank God for the contribution it has made to the educating forces of the race ; for the good it has been prompted to do ; for the part it had strength to play in the grandest drama of our generation ; and then, with our eyes lifted, and not dimmed by tears, we shall be able to say, out of a full heart, " Thou doest all things well. Blessed be Thy name ! Blessed be Thy name for the three-score overflowing years ; for the sunny sky she was permitted finally to see — the hated name made immortal — the periled life guarded by a nation's gratitude ; for the capstone put on with shoutings ; that she was privileged to enter the promised land and rest in the triumph, with the family circle unbroken — all she loved about her ! And blessed be Thy name, Father, that in due time, with gracious and tender loving-kindness, Thou didst break the bonds that hindered her true life, and take her to higher service in thine immediate presence ! "

RETURN TO ➡ **CIRCULATION DEPARTMENT**
202 Main Library

LOAN PERIOD 1 **HOME USE**	2	3
4	5	6

ALL BOOKS MAY BE RECALLED AFTER 7 DAYS
Renewals and Recharges may be made 4 days prior to the due date.
Books may be Renewed by calling 642-3405.

DUE AS STAMPED BELOW

OCT 0 3 1988		
AUTO DIS. SEP 11 '88		
JUL 16 1989		
aug. 14		
AUTO. DISC.		
JUL 1 9 1989		
CIRCULATION		

UNIVERSITY OF CALIFORNIA, BERKELEY
BERKELEY, CA 94720

FORM NO. DD6